# Amazing Mysteries
# UNSOLVED CRIMES

John Townsend

A+

**Smart Apple Media**

Smart Apple Media
P.O. Box 3263, Mankato, MN 56002

Printed in the United States of America

Library of Congress Cataloging-in-Publication Data

Townsend, John, 1955-
  Unsolved crimes / John Townsend.
     p. cm. --  (Amazing mysteries)
  Includes index.
  ISBN 978-1-59920-367-6 (hardcover)
  1.  Crime--Case studies--Juvenile literature. 2.  Murder--Investigation--Case studies--Juvenile literature.  I. Title.
  HV6251.T69 2010
  364.1--dc22
                              2008049938


Created by Q2AMedia
Editor: Jean Coppendale
Art Director: Rahul Dhiman
Designers: Harleen Mehta, Shilpi Sarkar
Picture Researcher: Shreya Sharma
Line Artist: Sibi N. Devasia
Coloring Artist: Mahender Kumar

All words in **bold** can be found in the glossary on pages 30–31.

Picture credits
t=top b=bottom c=center l=left r=right

Cover Image: Oliver Frey/ The Bridgeman Art Library/ Getty Images, Inset: Q2AMedia

Insides: Oliver Frey/ The Bridgeman Art Library/ Getty Images: 4r, Dic Liew/ Shutterstock: 5l, Mary Evans Picture Library/
Photolibrary: 6r, Ianni Dimitrov/Alamy: 8, Ho New/ Reuters: 9l, Everett Collection/ Rex Feature: 12-13,  Hulton Archive/ Stringer/
Getty Images: 13r, Demonoid/ iStockphoto: 14r, Bettmann/ Corbis: 15b,www.celebrateboston.com: 17, Time & Life Pictures/ Getty
Images: 18r, Joson/ Zefa/ Corbis: 19t, KennStilger/ Shutterstock: 20-21, Alexsl/ iStockphoto: 21,Newspix/ Rex Features: 22r, Simon
King/ Nature Picture Library:23r, Karl Gehring/ Liaison / Getty Images: 25b,Sipa Press/ Rex Features: 26, Mario Anzuoni-Pool/ Getty
Images: 27m, Emin Kuliyev/ Shutterstock: 28b, Michael Donne/ Photolibrary: 29r.

Q2A Media Art Bank: Title Page, 7, 9, 10, 11, 16, 24, 31.


9  8  7  6  5  4  3  2  1

# Contents

# The Perfect Crime

In the past, the police had very little equipment to help them solve crimes. Today, the latest science and technology can quickly collect, sort, and analyze all the **evidence**. But many crimes still go unsolved.

## The Perfect Murder?

Most killers hope to get away with murder. To do this they may try to hide the body or cover their tracks. By getting rid of all the evidence, a killer hopes to avoid getting caught. But the best plans can go wrong. Even when the victim is eaten by a shark, the police might still find out.

## CRIME FILE

**Crime:** Murder

**Victim:** James Smith

**Date:** 1935

**Place:** Australia

**Suspect:** Patrick Brady

! You might think throwing a body in the ocean is a good way of getting rid of it . . . not always!

# True Mystery

In 1935, a killer threw his victim into the sea so sharks would eat the evidence. But when a shark was caught and put in a tank at a zoo, the evidence suddenly turned up. In front of a crowd, the shark coughed up a man's left arm—with a tattoo on it! Fingerprints taken from the hand told police the body was a crook named James Smith, who had been reported missing. A **suspect** was arrested, but nothing could be proven. The case remains unsolved.

! Three big questions must be answered to solve any crime: Who did it? How? Why?

## UNSOLVED

Try being a detective. You arrive at a crime scene. It's a dark room with a body on the floor. The doors and windows are locked. The air vent is too small for anyone to get through. There's no sign of violence. How had the victim been killed? Find out on page 29.

# Invisible Weapon

The favorite murder weapon for hundreds of years was silent, secret, and difficult to trace—poison. The killer could pass it to the victim without a struggle and didn't even have to be there when the victim died—perfect!

## Terrible Pain

In 1857, Frenchman Emile L'Angelier was staying in Glasgow, Scotland. As he returned to his lodgings late one evening, he gripped his stomach. He fell into his room in terrible pain. The next day he was dead. His landlady immediately called the police.

! Emile arrived at his lodgings in great pain. Had he been poisoned?

## A Suspect

Emile's girlfriend was Madeleine Smith, but she had just ended their friendship. Madeleine now planned to marry another man. The police said she must have killed Emile to get him out of the way. The police found letters from Madeleine in Emile's room. They also found out that Madeleine had been to a pharmacy—to buy **arsenic**. She said it was to kill some rats. She also said she washed with it, as the deadly poison was thought to be good for the skin! But the police thought she had poisoned her ex-boyfriend.

### CRIME FILE

**Crime:** Murder

**Victim:** Emile L'Angelier

**Date:** 1857

**Place:** Glasgow, Scotland

**Suspect:** Madeleine Smith

### WHAT'S THE EVIDENCE?

- Madeleine planned to marry another man.
- She bought poison.
- Emile had been with Madeleine the night he died.

## Big News Story

Madeleine Smith was charged with murder and went to court. It seemed she would be found guilty. But the jury at her trial said the case couldn't be proven, so she had to be set free. She later married and moved away. No one knows what happened to Madeleine next. She was never heard from again.

**!** Did Madeleine add arsenic to Emile's drink when he wasn't looking?

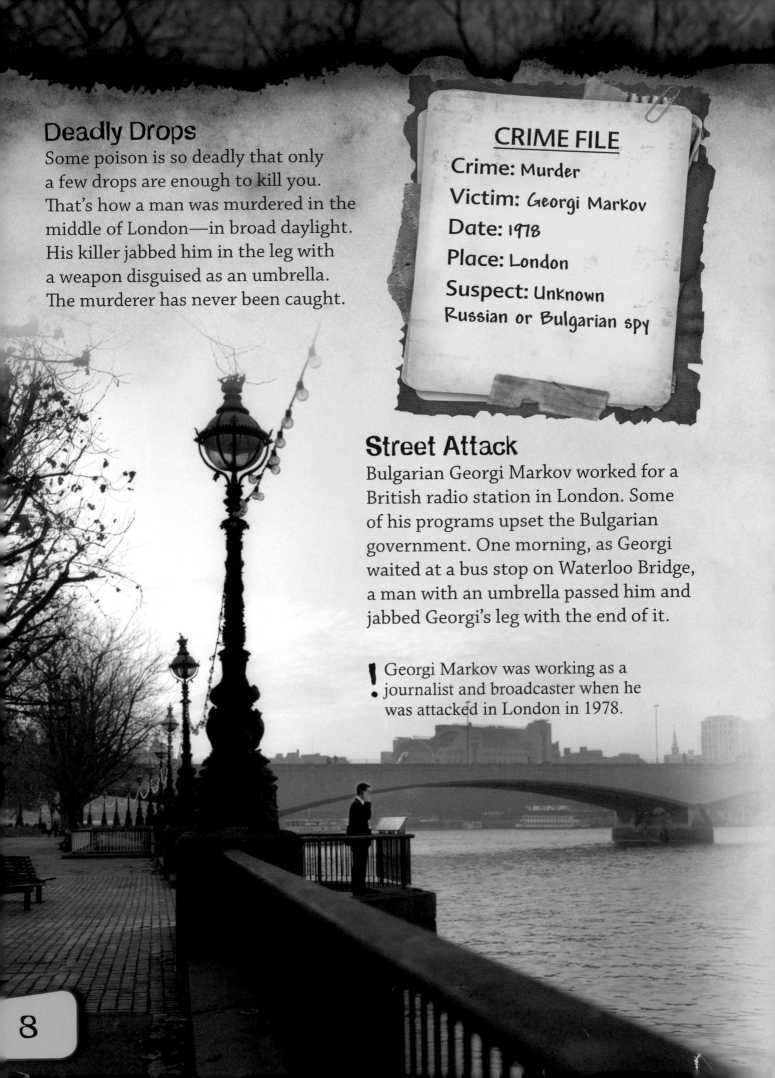

## Deadly Drops

Some poison is so deadly that only a few drops are enough to kill you. That's how a man was murdered in the middle of London—in broad daylight. His killer jabbed him in the leg with a weapon disguised as an umbrella. The murderer has never been caught.

**CRIME FILE**

Crime: Murder

Victim: Georgi Markov

Date: 1978

Place: London

Suspect: Unknown Russian or Bulgarian spy

## Street Attack

Bulgarian Georgi Markov worked for a British radio station in London. Some of his programs upset the Bulgarian government. One morning, as Georgi waited at a bus stop on Waterloo Bridge, a man with an umbrella passed him and jabbed Georgi's leg with the end of it.

! Georgi Markov was working as a journalist and broadcaster when he was attacked in London in 1978.

## Slow Death

Georgi Markov was in pain, but he went to work and told his friends what had happened. His leg began to swell and he saw spots of blood on his jeans. That evening he felt ill and soon had a high fever. By the next day he could hardly speak. He went to a hospital, where doctors thought he had blood poisoning. Georgi's body began to fail, and a few days later he was dead.

! Could the Bulgarian secret service and the Russian KGB have been behind the murder of Georgi Markov?

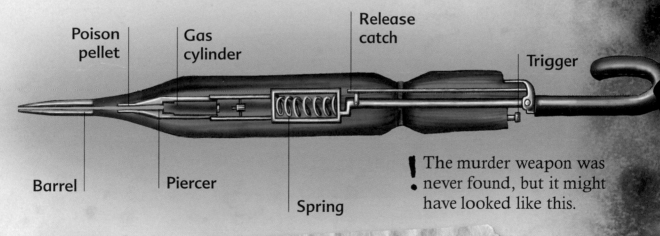

Poison pellet    Gas cylinder    Release catch    Trigger

Barrel    Piercer    Spring

! The murder weapon was never found, but it might have looked like this.

## UNSOLVED

Before Georgi died in the hospital, he managed to tell the police what had happened to him. His story seemed very far-fetched. When an **autopsy** was carried out, it showed that Georgi had been killed with a tiny pellet of **ricin**—one of the most lethal poisons known. But we're still not sure who actually killed him.

# Terror on the Streets

The autumn fog swirled over the cobbles and alleys of Victorian London. Gas lamps hissed and flickered in the damp darkness. Suddenly, a blood-curdling scream filled the night.

## Victorian Serial Killer

Fear was spreading through the streets of London. Could it be another murder? Over four months in 1888, five women in Whitechapel in the East End of London were attacked by the same vicious killer. Newspapers gave the murderer the name "Jack the Ripper."

## Afraid of the Dark

As stories of the terrible murders spread, people became afraid to go out at night. From their investigation, the police decided that the Ripper was a white male of average height between 20 and 40 years old.

Who was the mystery killer who stalked the streets of Victorian London? The police reported that the Ripper was not a "working man."

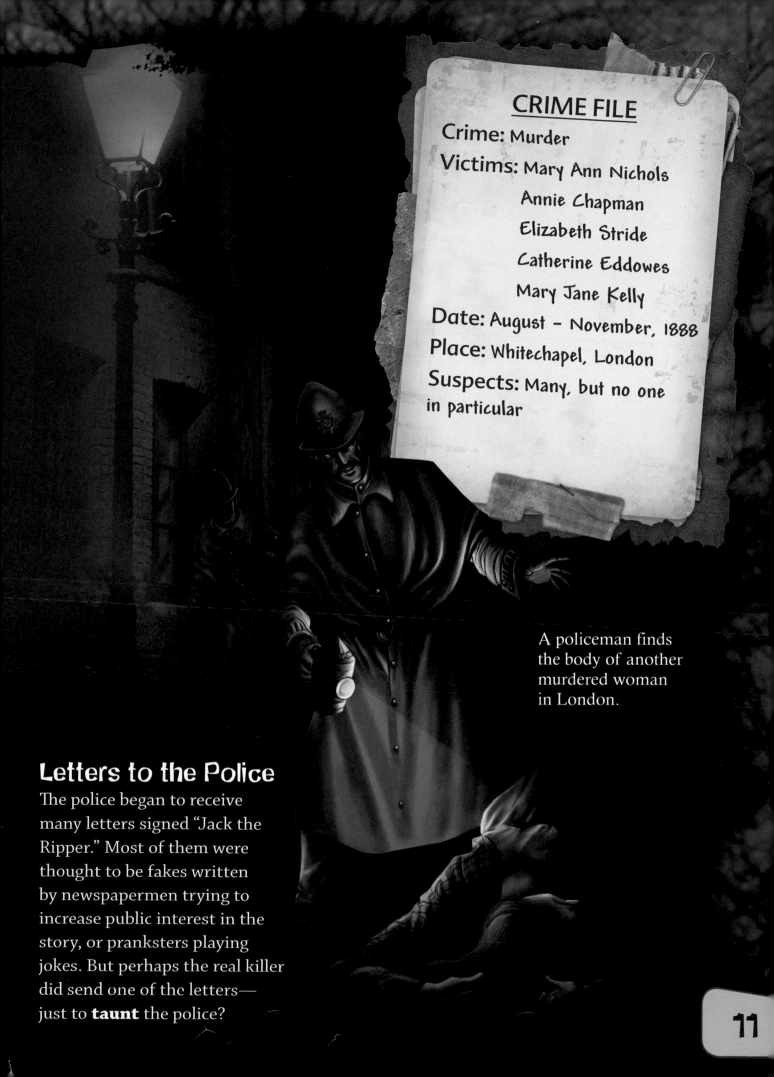

**CRIME FILE**

**Crime:** Murder

**Victims:** Mary Ann Nichols

Annie Chapman

Elizabeth Stride

Catherine Eddowes

Mary Jane Kelly

**Date:** August – November, 1888

**Place:** Whitechapel, London

**Suspects:** Many, but no one in particular

A policeman finds the body of another murdered woman in London.

## Letters to the Police

The police began to receive many letters signed "Jack the Ripper." Most of them were thought to be fakes written by newspapermen trying to increase public interest in the story, or pranksters playing jokes. But perhaps the real killer did send one of the letters— just to **taunt** the police?

## Killer Doctor?

The Ripper murders took place at a time before fingerprinting or **forensic science**. The only way the police could prove that someone was a murderer was either to catch him in the act or to get a suspect to confess. But the police were sure of something—the Ripper's victims all had knife wounds that showed the killer was right-handed and possibly a medical expert. The five victims all had similar wounds that could only have been made by someone with a knowledge of human **anatomy**.

 Every woman's biggest fear was being followed by the Ripper.

## EYE WITNESS

*Annie Chapman was the second victim of Jack the Ripper. She was 47 years old, in poor health, and had no money. A neighbor last saw her alive on Hanbury Street at about 5:30 a.m. talking to a man who may have been her killer. Annie Chapman's body was found 20 minutes later near a doorway in a backyard.*

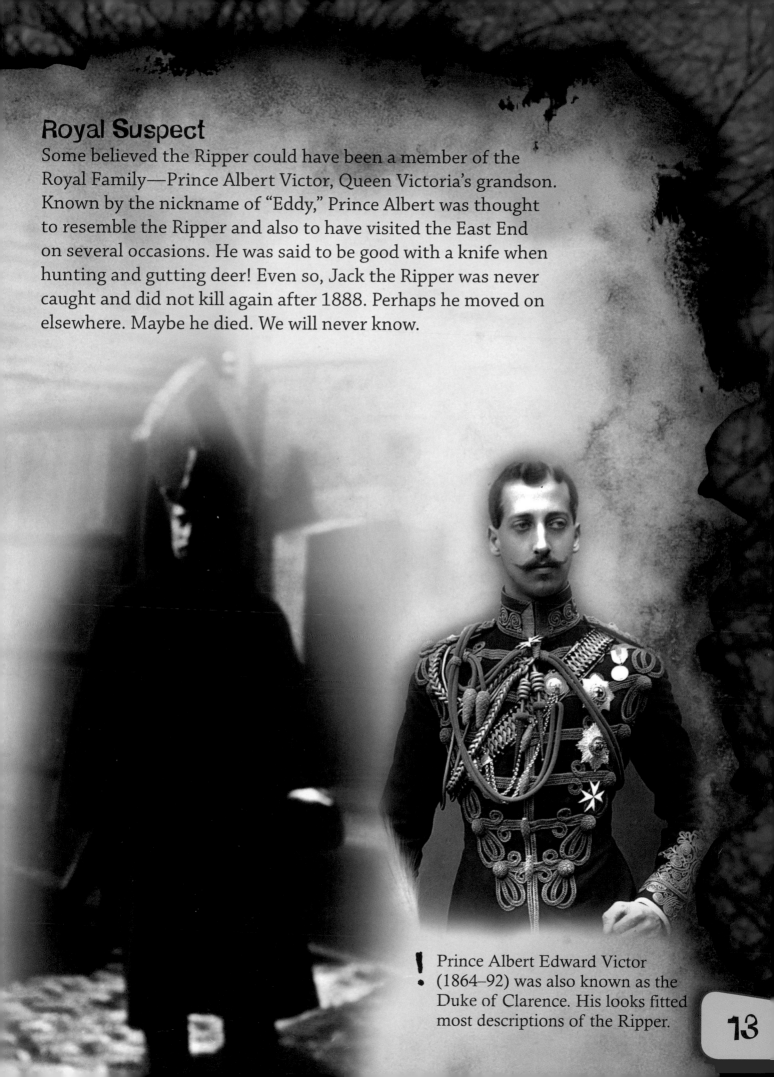

## Royal Suspect

Some believed the Ripper could have been a member of the Royal Family—Prince Albert Victor, Queen Victoria's grandson. Known by the nickname of "Eddy," Prince Albert was thought to resemble the Ripper and also to have visited the East End on several occasions. He was said to be good with a knife when hunting and gutting deer! Even so, Jack the Ripper was never caught and did not kill again after 1888. Perhaps he moved on elsewhere. Maybe he died. We will never know.

! Prince Albert Edward Victor
• (1864–92) was also known as the Duke of Clarence. His looks fitted most descriptions of the Ripper.

# Axe Murders

A murder mystery in the 1890s became famous all over the United States and was soon the theme for a children's nursery rhyme. But we still don't know who committed the grisly axe murders.

## Murder in the House

Lizzie Borden was a single woman and a Sunday school teacher in New England. At the age of 34, she and her older sister still lived with their father and stepmother. One August morning in 1892, Lizzie found her father murdered. He had been killed with an axe. Lizzie ran next door to get help, as her sister was away at the time.

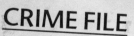

### CRIME FILE

**Crime:** Murder

**Victims:** Andrew and Abby Borden

**Date:** 1892

**Place:** New England

**Suspect:** Lizzie Borden

THE CURSE OF
# LIZZIE
# BORDEN

! The chilling axe murders in Massachusetts gripped the country.

## Main Suspect

While Lizzie was next door, the maid brought more news. She'd just found Lizzie's stepmother—also killed with an axe. Lizzie was the main suspect. After all, she had been the only other member of the family in the house at the time, and it was known she and her parents had been arguing a lot. Had she snapped and taken an axe to her father and stepmother? The police thought so.

## On Trial for Murder

The following year Lizzie was arrested and went to court to be tried for both murders. The jury was unable to **convict** her for murder due to a lack of evidence. During the entire ordeal, Lizzie Borden remained very calm and in control. People refused to believe that a wealthy Sunday school teacher would kill her parents. The police felt sure she was the killer. There were no other suspects.

! The Borden house in
Fall River, Massachusetts,
where the murders took place.

### WHAT'S THE EVIDENCE?

If Lizzie had been the killer, she would have been covered with blood. She wasn't. In fact, no blood-soaked clothing was found at the crime scene. But a few days after the murder, Lizzie tore up a blue cotton dress and burned it in the kitchen stove. She said she'd brushed against wet paint. But was she trying to get rid of evidence?

## Motive for Murder

Why would quiet Lizzie want to kill her father and his wife? What people didn't know at the time was that Lizzie's father had threatened to cut her out of his will. After the murder, Lizzie **inherited** half of her father's estate and bought a mansion for herself and her sister, Emma, in an expensive neighborhood. Strangely, Emma soon moved away and never spoke to Lizzie again. No one knows why.

## Axe Murderer?

The Borden House at 92 Second Street had a barn behind it, where Lizzie claimed she had been working at the time of the murders. Maybe she lost her temper after an earlier fight with her father and ran indoors waving the axe.

Children at the time heard the story about Lizzie, and they made up this grisly rhyme:

*Lizzie Borden took an axe*
*And gave her mother forty whacks.*
*And when she saw what she had done*
*She gave her father forty-one.*

No one could believe the respectable Lizzie Borden would kill her rich father and stepmother with an axe.

## Secrets to the Grave

Lizzie continued to live in her grand house until her death in 1927, at the age of 67. She was buried near her parents in the Oak Grove Cemetery at Fall River. Lizzie never confessed to being a murderer. No one else was ever arrested or tried for the murder of Abby and Andrew Borden.

! Lizzie Borden's house is now a guest house, and people pay to sleep in her room! Would you?

## UNSOLVED

What the jury never heard was that on the day before the murders, Lizzie tried to buy poison (**cyanide**) from a pharmacist. No one knows why. In the trial, the pharmacist wasn't called to give evidence.

# The Robber Who Disappeared

It was an amazing crime—an unknown robber jumped from a plane with a hoard of money and was never found. How could a man acting alone manage to **hijack** a large aircraft and steal so much money and get away with it?

## Ordinary Man

The man wore a nice suit and tie and looked very ordinary. He carried a suitcase and had sunglasses. He bought a ticket for a one-way flight from Portland to Seattle, using the name D. B. Cooper. It was November, 1971. Who Mr. Cooper really was remains a mystery. What happened to him is also a mystery. He committed an incredible crime that still baffles the FBI after 40 years.

**CRIME FILE**

Crime: Hijack and robbery

Victim: An airline

Date: 1971

Place: Seattle

Suspect: Still uncertain

! This is how the hijacker might have looked.

## Demand for Money

After the plane had taken off, Cooper handed a note to the steward saying he had a bomb. He demanded $200,000. He said the crew had to land in Seattle and pick up the money and four parachutes. They did everything he asked, to avoid panic. In Seattle, the passengers got off the plane unaware of what was happening. Cooper demanded the plane take off again with just the crew and himself on board.

### EYE WITNESS

*Two flight attendants were interviewed separately on the night of the crime. They gave similar descriptions of the thief. He was 5'10" to 6' (1.78 to 1.83 m) tall and in his mid-40s, with brown eyes.*

## Parachute Jump

Having tied all the bills to his body, and with a parachute on his back, Cooper jumped from the plane! He was 2 miles (3 km) up and the night was freezing. The windchill was -71°F (-57°C) and it was pouring rain. Experts said he could not survive the cold in ordinary clothes. Yet he and the money disappeared—and Cooper was never seen again.

## Lost Money

In 1980, a boy found nearly $6,000 by the Columbia River. Cooper had jumped from the plane somewhere above this river nine years earlier. The bills matched those stolen by Cooper. But what happened to the rest? Maybe Cooper landed safely and spent it, or maybe he was killed in the jump.

## No Expert

The police were certain Cooper was not an expert skydiver. No one in their right mind would have jumped out of a plane at night, in the rain, with a 200 mph (320 km/h) wind in his face—it was far too risky. He also didn't see that his reserve parachute had been sewn shut. A skilled skydiver would have checked it.

! The mystery hijacker could have landed anywhere here. The police are still baffled. No body or bones have ever been found.

### WHAT'S THE EVIDENCE?

During the hijacking, Cooper wore a black tie, which he removed before jumping. In 2001, the police used it to get a **DNA** sample. So far it has matched no known criminal.

## Possible Suspects

A man called Richard McCoy was once thought to be Cooper, but he died in 1974 before **DNA** tests were used. However, it turned out he looked nothing like the hijacker and was at home the day after the hijacking. Then, in 2000, a woman in Florida said her dying husband confessed to being Cooper—but his DNA did not match that on Cooper's tie.

## Open File

The FBI is keeping the Cooper file open and still asks the public for help. They want to know where Cooper landed that night. Did he fall in the Colombia River? Diving into the wilderness without a plan, without the right equipment, in such terrible conditions, he probably never even got his parachute open—but we may never know.

### UNSOLVED

"It's a mystery, frankly. We've run down thousands of leads and considered all sorts of **scenarios**. Yet the case remains unsolved. Would we still like to get our man? Absolutely."—The FBI.

# The Dingo Baby Mystery

A tragic story from Australia made world news in 1980. A baby just nine-and-a-half weeks old disappeared while the family was on a camping trip. Her mother went on trial for killing her.

## A Cry in the Night

Lindy and Michael Chamberlain were camping at **Uluru (Ayers Rock)** in Australia. One of their sons and their baby daughter were asleep in a tent while Lindy was nearby. People told her they heard a baby cry.

## CRIME FILE

**Crime:** Possible kidnap and murder

**Victim:** Azaria Chamberlain

**Date:** 1980

**Place:** Uluru, Australia

**Suspects:** Lindy Chamberlain; A dingo

! Michael and Lindy Chamberlain at Uluru, Australia showing police officers the area where their baby disappeared.

## Horror!

When Lindy reached the tent, she saw a large wild dog beside it. It was a **dingo**, and it looked as if it was dragging something. Lindy couldn't see what it was at first, but suddenly she realized what it might be. She ran into the tent and stared in horror at Azaria's empty bed. Lindy screamed into the night, "A dingo took my baby!"

! A dingo could easily kill a small baby.

## Gone for Good

Azaria was never seen again. The police found no sign of the missing baby. Soon rumors began to spread. Surely a dingo wouldn't steal a baby? The police began to think Lindy must have killed and hidden her own baby. They charged her with her baby's murder. Then, in 1986, police found a piece of Azaria's clothing near a dingo's lair at Uluru. Perhaps Lindy was innocent after all? After serving three years in prison, Lindy was set free.

## UNSOLVED

For some reason, the police had doubts about the dingo explanation. Although Lindy Chamberlain was sent to prison for killing her baby, many people thought she was innocent. There was no real proof. After a long campaign to have her name cleared, a special court decided Lindy was not Azaria's killer after all and cleared her of any guilt. Lindy was set free. But exactly what happened to baby Azaria remains a mystery.

# Kidnap or Murder?

In 1996, a news story stunned the United States—a six-year-old girl named JonBenet Ramsey had disappeared from her bed at 5:52 a.m. Her mother called the police and said she'd found a **ransom** note saying JonBenet had been kidnapped.

> ### RANSOM NOTE:
> You will withdraw $118,000 from your account. $100,000 will be in $100 bills and the remaining $18,000 in $20 bills. Make sure that you bring a big enough case to the bank. When you get home you will put the money in a brown paper bag. I will call you between 8 and 10 a.m. tomorrow to instruct you.

JonBenet Ramsey (1990–96). Her family has been cleared of the murder, but who did commit this terrible crime?

## Mother Under Suspicion

For a while JonBenet's own mother was a suspect. The ransom note was written on paper that belonged to the Ramsey family. A felt-tip pen similar to the one used to write the note was found in the kitchen. A practice sheet for the ransom note was found on the same pad of paper. However, in 2008 new DNA tests finally proved that JonBenet's family was not involved in this terrible crime.

## A Murder Scene

The local police had a quick look around the house and yard. There was no sign of a break-in. Later, JonBenet's father searched the basement and found her body under a blanket. The house was now a murder scene.

## WHAT'S THE EVIDENCE?

🔍 An autopsy showed JonBenet had been strangled with a rope. Her skull had also been fractured. She had eaten pineapple a few hours before the murder, but her mother said there was no pineapple in the house. Yet photographs from the day JonBenet's body was found showed a bowl of pineapple on the kitchen table. Her parents didn't remember putting this bowl on the table.

## Damaged Evidence

No one had realized the house was a murder scene, so objects were moved before they could be photographed. Family, friends, and police had roamed about freely. JonBenet's parents picked up her body and disturbed any evidence. As it was Christmas, police experts did not arrive for six hours. It had been at least 14 hours since JonBenet had died, or maybe longer. The exact time of her death could never be proven.

❗ The Ramseys' home became a crime scene, surrounded by Christmas decorations.

## Looking for the Killer

The police were not used to this sort of crime in such a quiet neighborhood. They were blamed for not treating the crime scene with enough care. They were also blamed for suspecting that JonBenet's parents and even her nine-year-old brother could be involved in the murder.

## WHAT'S THE EVIDENCE?

There were clues that an **intruder** had been in the house:

- Two footprints in the basement did not match any of the shoes in the house.
- A third footprint of an unknown person was on the outer part of the window near the basement.
- A rope was found on the bed in a room near JonBenet's room.

## Moving On

In 2003, a judge said the murder of JonBenet was probably the work of an intruder. The family was no longer under suspicion. In fact, a DNA sample on JonBenet's body didn't match any known suspect or member of the family.

! JonBenet often appeared in glamorous clothes at pageants and shows.

## Strange Confession

Then, ten years after the murder, 41-year-old John Karr was arrested after he sent emails to a journalist saying he knew about the Ramsey murder. John Karr confessed to being with JonBenet when she died, saying her death was an accident. However, his DNA did not match that found on JonBenet's body. For some reason, Karr had made up his story.

**!** John Karr in court

### UNSOLVED

The murder of JonBenet Ramsey has never been solved. JonBenet's mother, Patsy Ramsey, died in 2006 at the age of 49, never knowing who killed her daughter. It may be a matter of time before the killer or killers are finally caught—or will this case remain yet another unsolved murder?

# The Search Continues

Crimes will always be full of mysteries, but modern technology is making it easier for the police to solve crimes—even some very old ones.

## DNA Breakthrough

Our body cells are **unique**, just like our fingerprints. They contain information that can be made into a **DNA profile**, and profiles from different DNA samples can be compared very accurately. If there's an exact match, it means both samples are from the same person. The first time DNA was used in solving a crime was in 1988.

## Solving with Science

Thousands of crimes have been solved using DNA evidence, including unsolved crimes committed many years ago, before DNA testing. **Databases** now hold millions of DNA profiles. Around 1,000 profiles are taken from crime scenes each week. Sometimes they match DNA taken from crime scenes many years ago.

! With modern science, even the most perfect murder could be solved eventually. Maybe some of the mysteries in this book will be solved one day by DNA testing.

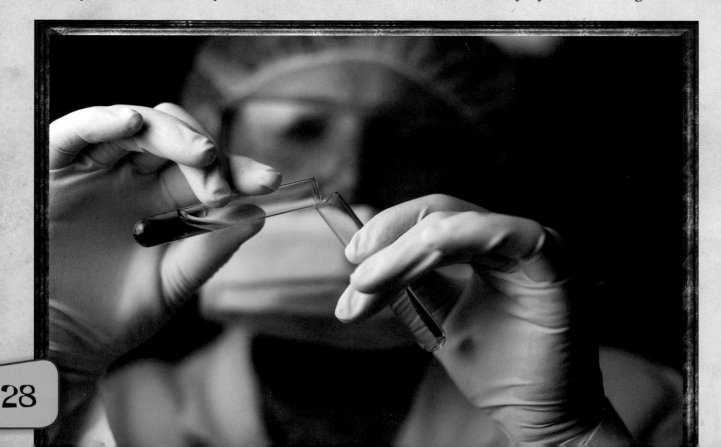

## DNA Match

Anita Carrier was 20 years old when she was murdered in 1976 in California. For more than 30 years, this remained an unsolved crime. But in 2008, DNA evidence solved the murder case. DNA from the murderer was found under the victim's fingernails. Computers finally matched it to a prisoner, Charles Manley. He had died in a Nevada prison in 2001 while awaiting execution for another murder. Even though he wasn't convicted for Anita's murder, her family at least knows the case is solved.

! Crime scene investigators at work.

## UNSOLVED

Did you work out how the victim was killed on page 5? The air vent was the clue. That was where the murderer pushed through the tube . . . before turning on the cyanide gas.

# Glossary

| | |
|---|---|
| anatomy | the study of the body, its organs, and working parts |
| arsenic | an extremely poisonous, white substance used especially in insecticides |
| autopsy | an examination of a dead body, especially to find out the cause of death |
| convict | to find guilty |
| cyanide | a highly poisonous substance |
| database | a collection of data (information) usually organized on computer records |
| dingo | a reddish-brown, bushy-tailed wild dog native to Australia |
| DNA | the special code in the center of each person's genes, or cells, that makes each person an individual |
| DNA profile | a pattern made by using DNA from cells that may be found at a crime scene, used to identify suspects |
| evidence | material presented to a court to help prove a legal case |
| forensic science | the study of detailed scientific information from a crime, which can be used in a court of law |
| hijack | to take over the control of a vehicle, such as an aircraft |
| inherit | to receive money or goods from a person when that person dies |
| intruder | someone who forces entry into a building without permission |

| | |
|---|---|
| ransom | something paid or demanded for the freedom of a captured person |
| ricin | an extremely poisonous substance made from the seeds of the castor oil plant |
| scenario | a sequence of events that make up a situation |
| suspect | a person thought to be guilty of a crime |
| taunt | to provoke or challenge in a mocking or insulting manner |
| Uluru (Ayers Rock) | a large outcrop of red rock in central Australia in SW Northern Territory |
| unique | the only one of its kind in the world |

# Index

# Web Finder

www.cyberbee.com/whodunnit/crime.html
Find out about forensic science by doing these simple experiments.

www.sciencenewsforkids.org/articles/20060503/Feature1.asp
Fascinating information about fingerprints and crime

http://kids.mysterynet.com
See if you can solve the mysteries on this site.

www.fbi.gov/page2/dec07/dbcooper123107.html
The FBI's official information page about the D. B. Cooper hijack mystery